galatians

A **SIMPLY BIBLE** STUDY

CARMEN BEASLEY

To our Savior, Jesus Christ,
who for freedom has set us free.

And to the women at
The Chapel in Green seeking
to stand firm in His freedom.

For freedom Christ has set us free;
stand firm therefore, and do not
submit again to a yoke of slavery.

GALATIANS 5:1

FOR FREEDOM
CHRIST HAS SET
US FREE...

GALATIANS 5:1

table of *contents*

GALATIANS | A **SIMPLY BIBLE** STUDY

NOW YOU, BROTHERS,
LIKE ISAAC, ARE
CHILDREN OF PROMISE.

GALATIANS 4:28

welcome!

SHARING GOD'S STORY OF **SIMPLY BIBLE**

AS A LITTLE GIRL, I ADORED COLORING BOOKS. Smooth, crisp, white pages displayed bold black lines of perfectly-drawn figures and characters. The spaces patiently awaited color. Fondly, I remember the joy of opening a new pack of crayons. The neat little rows of pointed tips colorfully peeked out and tantalized me as if to say, "Try to choose just one!" Creativity awaited. Or so I thought.

When my four children were small, through a friend of a friend, I was encouraged to forgo coloring books. My initial reaction was one of horror. "What? Coloring books are fun! That would be forgoing fun! Plain paper? How boring!" Okay, granted… my reaction was a little melodramatic, but I do remember thinking these thoughts.

Instead, this friend insisted that providing children with blank sheets of paper was the way to spur creativity. I could see the wisdom. Not to mention, a ream of paper was way cheaper than four new coloring books… and so, I gave it a try. For the most part, my children simply grew up with lots of plain white paper and a variety of colorful pencils, crayons, and markers.

SIMPLE TOOLS LED TO ARTISTRY. My kids learned to draw. Not just little stick figures in the middle of the page, but they learned to tell a story using a piece of paper. Masterpieces. (At least in my eyes!)

Now I'm sure no one ever saved one of my coloring book pages. Oh, for sure! Sometimes one landed on Grandma's refrigerator. However, right now, down in my basement, binders of pictures remain—pictures that my budding artists created more than twenty years ago. Why? These pictures were windows into their little hearts and minds. These illustrations tell stories. And this mom treasures them in her heart.

THIS IS THE GIST OF **SIMPLY BIBLE**. My heart desires to provide women with a "blank page" for reading and engaging with God and His Word. Rather than fill-in-the-blank questions, this study offers space to observe, understand, and apply. Don't get me wrong: just like coloring books, traditional Bible studies have their place. I wouldn't be the Bible student that I am today without them. And yet, I am rather fond of this series. Basic tools and gentle direction allow for a quiet place where women are able to engage their hearts, souls, and minds with the intention of listening to and knowing God. It's a place for women to relate and retreat with Him by sharing in His story—simply the Bible.

TO BE HONEST, **SIMPLY BIBLE** ALMOST DIDN'T HAPPEN. Yep! I've shared this story before, but here it goes again. It's sort of embarrassing.

After much prayer as a newly-appointed women's ministry director of my church, I was assessing the state of our women's ministries when God pointed me toward inductive Bible study. Inductive study implies investigating the Bible directly. That's it. And so, in my mind, the conversation looked like this:

> **Me:** "Lord, You mean no video teaching and no fill-in-the-blank workbooks?

> **God:** "Yes. Take women directly to my Word."

> **Me:** "Lord, women like to have a book in their hands, and preferably one from a well-known author."

> **God:** "Use my Book."

So then, I obeyed. Ugh! I wish had immediately obeyed. Instead, and this is the embarrassing part, I played Gideon. I set my fleece out for God to prove His point, and I did it more than once. (If at this point you're doubting the validity of an author and a women's ministry leader who plays Gideon, I understand. You are welcome to return this book, no questions asked!) Instead of obeying, I purchased and reviewed every single Bible study available, at that time, on the gospel of John. Almost desperately, I was searching for something—anything—that would quietly and inductively walk women through that Gospel. One by one, God said "no." (Okay, it's not like God audibly spoke to me. But His Spirit has a way of getting His message across. You know what I mean?)

I continued to cry out to Him for a tool. Frankly, for years, as an experienced leader and Bible teacher, I had searched for a simple tool that does not require in-depth or extra training in order to teach or study inductively. I could not find one.

One day, while wrestling and praying over all of this, I sat down at my computer, opened a blank document, and began experimenting with the process of inductive study. I left my computer and went down to fix dinner. When I returned, I looked at what was on the paper and thought, "This works." Praise God! In perfect timing, He granted peace and direction.

He also led the way to Melissa Trew, a talented designer with a huge heart for God and His Word. She's a gift. Deftly, she takes this material, uses her God-giftedness, and turns it into something beautiful. Coffee-table worthy. Her designs are beyond anything I could begin to think or imagine. I'm grateful.

FINALLY, WHY INDUCTIVE STUDY? There are three main reasons, based on what today's woman says about Bible study:

FIRST: *"I feel inept. I know I should read the Bible. I want to, but I don't understand it."* Many women feel the same. With an influx of Bible study resources, we have relied on videos and books that give us the author's answers. It's easy to think we need an "expert" to intercede and interpret God's Word on our behalf. No doubt, there is a place for these resources, but we aren't to be dependent on them. We depend on God alone.

An old Chinese Proverb aptly says:

> Give a man a fish and you feed him for a day.
> Teach a man to fish and you feed him for a lifetime.

SIMPLY BIBLE is designed to equip women to "fish." By following the step-by-step framework, you can confidently approach God's Word. The inductive process of this journal eliminates my voice as much as possible, with the hopes that you can listen to God's voice alone. That's the beauty of inductive study: rather than listening to *an* author, we listen directly to *the* Author. My prayer is that, through His Word, we will experience the incredible joy and adventure of personal encounters with Him. And then? We share Him with others.

SECOND: *"I'm busy. Overwhelmed by demands. Life is crazy!"*
I know. I feel it too. This study should maximize time. Rather than spending time reading other books, watching videos, filling in the blanks, and checking Bible study off our "to-do" list, we skip the "middle-man" and go directly to God and His Word. Immediately, we relate with Him one-on-one.

Truly, this study can be catered to the needs of the busy woman who can barely scrape together ten minutes a day for Bible study. Yet, it can also fit the need of the woman who longs to linger and dig deeper into the Word. Kind of like scuba diving, you'll choose how deep you want to go and how far you'd like to roam.

THIRD: *"I need relationship. Do others care about me?"*
Today's younger woman is seeking connection. Her desire? To be seen, known, and loved. Video teaching often does not meet her expressed need because it takes time away from deeper relationship-building—both with Christ and with others. Although she is hungry to know, the bottom line is that she prefers personal interaction. And the discussion had better be relevant and meaningful, with no pat answers.

Concurringly, a generation of women my age is now dependent on video teachers and fill-in-the-blank studies, rather than dependent on God and His Word. Because of her dependency on these tools, a veteran Bible student is often ill-equipped to read the Bible for herself and even more ill-equipped to share her faith and God's Word with others.

Inductive study maximizes time and develops skills to focus on real relationship and interaction with God and others. Why **SIMPLY BIBLE**? To focus on the "relationship need" now felt acutely within women's ministries across the country.

CONSIDER FAST FOOD VERSUS A HOME-COOKED MEAL. Picking up fast food can be a treat. It's quick and easy. It's downright helpful to have someone else prepare and hand you the meal. Much of our Bible study resources are similar to "fast food." Someone else does the preparation and serves up a quick and easy word of encouragement. It's helpful, but it's not "home-cooked." Rarely would we serve fast food to friends or carry it to a potluck. The same holds true for feasting on God's Word. Inductive study allows for that special and intimate meal meant to be shared with others.

SO THAT'S A GOD-AT-WORK STORY. That's how **SIMPLY BIBLE** was birthed.

Since its inception, I've had the joy and privilege of watching women journal and seek God through these study workbooks. These journals are windows into hearts, souls, and minds growing with God. These notebooks tell stories. And although they are much too private for me to observe closely, I treasure them in my heart. If I could, I'd pile them up in my basement.

For each woman who has braved a **SIMPLY BIBLE** study, I am truly grateful. In a sense, there is a basement in my heart where memories of studying with you are tucked away. Thank you. You spur me on to dig deep into God's Word, to know and love Him and others more deeply.

If you are new, you've probably gathered by now that this study is different. And different often falls outside our comfort zones. The purpose of this journal is that you may confidently read, understand, and apply God's Word like you've never before experienced, using *simply* the Bible. It will require a commitment.

COMMIT. There's no "Oh, I'll just give it a try." Commit to see this study through to the finish.

If the inductive Bible study process is new to you, don't be intimidated. My first home-cooked meal didn't look or taste anything like my mom's meal. Cooking takes practice. Even after forty some years of cooking, most of what I cook tastes different from my mom's cooking. The same will be true for Bible study. Inductive study will take practice. Your study will look different from most others. You are unique and special. And so, your study insights and application will be unique. But, by the end, you will better know Jesus Christ, His Word, and your identity in Him. You are loved, valued, and treasured by an amazing God.

SO WELCOME TO **SIMPLY BIBLE**! And welcome to this particular series of Galatians, Ephesians, Philippians, and Colossians.

These epistles (or letters), written by the Apostle Paul, share a window into a heart set free to fully know and seek God. As we engage and share in God's Word, like Paul, may we yield our hearts and minds to God's heart, having the mind of Christ Jesus. And may He permeate and etch His fruit of love, joy, peace, patience, kindness, goodness, faithfulness, gentleness, and self-control onto the pages of our own hearts, for His glory.

I'm praying for you and with you.

With much love and joy,

getting *started*

A QUICK-START GUIDE TO **SIMPLY BIBLE**

...WE KNOW THAT A PERSON
IS NOT JUSTIFIED BY WORKS
OF THE LAW BUT THROUGH
FAITH IN JESUS CHRIST...

GALATIANS 2:16

getting *started*

AN INTRODUCTION TO INDUCTIVE BIBLE STUDY

Recently, a friend described **SIMPLY BIBLE** as "leaving behind her paint-by-numbers set for a blank canvas." Of course, her word picture melted my heart! But honestly, whether painting or digging into God's Word, using a blank canvas can be a little intimidating. It takes practice! Just as an artist learns a particular method and handles special tools to create a masterpiece, so do Bible study students.

The inductive Bible study method involves three basic steps that often overlap:
> **(1)** Observe
> **(2)** Interpret
> **(3)** Apply

Using the **SIMPLY BIBLE** format will help to paint a more thorough understanding of God's Word.

On the following pages, you will find a quick-start guide to **SIMPLY BIBLE**. This guide is followed by a more thorough explanation of the format and basic study tools. Take time to get a feel for them.

And then... dig in!

a quick start to *simply bible*

A STEP-BY-STEP GUIDE

READ	OBSERVE	INTERPRET
Read the passage. Try some of the following ideas to help you read carefully. (Highlighters and colored pencils are fun here!)	As you read, write down your observations in this column. Simply notice what the Scripture *says*. This is your place for notes. Ideas include:	In this column, record what the passage *means*.
• Read the passage in a different version.	• Ask questions of the text, like "who, what, when, where, or how."	One way to interpret is to answer any questions asked during observation. Try to first answer these *without* the aid of other helps. Allow Scripture to explain Scripture. It often does.
• Read it out loud.	• Jot down key items: people, places, things. Mark places on a map.	If the answers are not intuitive or easily found near the passage, other tools are available. Use boxes A, B, and C to identify a key word, define it, and look up a cross reference. This extra research will shed light on the meaning.
• Underline, circle, box, or highlight repeated words, unfamiliar words, or anything that catches your attention.	• Ask, "What does this Scripture passage say about Jesus?"	
• Listen to the passage while running errands.	• Note what took place before and after this passage.	IMPORTANT: Seek to understand what the passage meant to the author and his original readers. Try to look at the world through the eyes of early Christians.
• Doodle or write out a verse in a journaling Bible.	• Ponder.	
	• Ask God if there is anything else He'd like you to notice.	

PLEASE NOTE: The following boxes (labeled A, B, and C) are interpretation tools. These are meant to be used in unison with the "Interpret" column on the previous page to aid in interpreting Scripture. Most women find it helpful to complete these *before* interpreting. Find what's most helpful for you.

A KEY WORDS	**B** DEFINITIONS	**C** CROSS REFERENCES
When you notice a word that is repeated multiple times, is unfamiliar, or is interesting to you in any other way, record it here.	Here, record definitions of your key words. You can find the appropriate definitions by using: • a Bible concordance (defines words according to the original language) • a Bible dictionary • another translation	Note cross references. This is a solid way to allow Scripture to interpret Scripture. If your Bible does not include cross references, they can be found easily using web-based Bible resources.

Bible study tools like those listed above can be found by visiting the following websites:

blueletterbible.org   biblegateway.com   biblehub.com

MAIN POINTS	APPLY
Summarize the main point(s) or note any themes you encountered in the passage.	Apply God's Word specifically to your own life. Application is personal. God may teach, correct, rebuke, or train. He is always equipping. (II Tim. 3:16-17) Record what this passage means to you.

PRAY
Write a short prayer here. When we take time to write something down, that message becomes more etched on our heart. Take a moment to simply be with God. He is why we study. Savor. Know. Praise. Confess. Thank. Ask. Love. Then carry a nugget of His Word in your heart to ponder and proclaim throughout your day.

CHRIST REDEEMED US
FROM THE CURSE OF
THE LAW BY BECOMING
A CURSE FOR US...

GALATIANS 3:13

step by *step*

UNPACKING THE INDUCTIVE METHOD

step by *step*

UNPACKING THE INDUCTIVE METHOD

STEPS 1 & 2: READ AND OBSERVE | *See what the Bible **says**.*
The first step to Bible study is simply reading God's Word.

The problem is that, in our hurried, scurried pace of life, we often plow right through it without taking time to ponder and think about what we're reading. *Observing* what we read helps us to slow down and take notice in order to see and answer, "What does the Bible *say*?"

Have you ever slowed down to truly examine and enjoy a piece of art? Artists have an amazing knack or ability to capture a particular scene, whether real or imagined, onto a blank canvas. How? Artists specialize in observing details. Setting, color, texture, time, characters, lighting, movement... the list of details is nearly limitless.

We can do this, too.

When they were young, blank sketch pads and new drawing pencils became a special treat for my children. Now imagine me with my small army of little ones traipsing off to a park with these tools in hand. Before pulling out a pencil to begin creating, the first thing to do was to find the right spot. (I highly recommend that for Bible study, too!) Then we'd observe.

To observe means "to see, watch, notice, or regard with attention, especially so as to see or learn something."[1] *Especially so as to see or learn something.*

And so, with my children, we would notice things. Lots of things! The different types of leaves, flowers, plants, grass, insects, animals, and more. Once engaged in observing, details begin to arise! How fun to zero in and observe the lady bug crawling along the

---

[1] **ethos**. Dictionary.com. *Dictionary.com Unabridged.* Random House, Inc. http://www.dictionary.com/browse/ethos (accessed: March 16, 2018).

blade of grass or the spots that adorn a toad sunning on the sidewalk or the veins that run throughout a maple leaf. There's so much to see!

Observation implies being curious. Noticing details. Asking questions.

Kids do this naturally. We can too. Be curious with God's Word. Scripture is full of details to notice and so many questions to ask. When we slow down to "smell the roses" within Scripture, we will see and learn something.

As you read, ask God's help to see what He would have you to see. Ask questions of the text and highlight verses that touch your heart. If anything is especially noteworthy to you, jot it down in the space to observe. (Keep in mind: this framework is simply a guide. You can fill in as little or as much of the space as you desire.)

The bottom line? Read. Read carefully. Then observe at least one thing. By doing so, we will see Scripture more clearly.

STEP 3: INTERPRET | *Understand what the Bible **means**.*

After careful observation of a landscape, an artist sketches an *interpretation* of what he sees onto the canvas. Observation and interpretation go hand in hand. A circle is a circle. A square is a square. As closely as possible, the artist defines and places an image of what he observes onto the canvas. Careful observation leads to a life-like rendering such that the viewer will enjoy a solid understanding of what the artist himself observed.

The same is true of the Bible. Observation and interpretation go hand in hand. Scripture will often interpret Scripture. As we carefully read and observe what the scripture says, we frequently understand and simultaneously interpret it's meaning. So, within our daily study format, observation and interpretation are located side-by-side.

One simple way to understand the meaning of Scripture is to answer any questions that we've asked of the text. Try answering them without the aid of study notes or other helps. Utilize scripture to interpret scripture.

Other times, interpretation is not so easy. After all, the Bible was written in ancient times, spanning the course of over 2,000 years, by a people and to a people of a culture that is utterly foreign to us.

Therefore, certain resources are handy. These tools help us to place and understand Scripture in its original context, in order to properly interpret what we've read. (Think of an artist pulling out a ruler—a simple tool that helps to more accurately reproduce a scene. A ruler is not necessary, but is useful.)

Bible study tools can include:

- *Cross references:* Cross references allow us to use nearby or related passages to more accurately interpret Scripture.
- *Bible dictionaries and concordances:* These tools allow us to understand the meaning of a word in its original language.
- *Bible handbooks and commentaries:* Resources like these help us to verify our conclusions as well as provide historical or cultural context.

It's important to remember that Scripture, in its original context, had only one meaning. Not multiple meanings. And although God can be mysterious, there are no mystical or hidden meanings within Scripture. Paul had a specific message, written at a specific time and in a specific place, for a specific group of people. He meant what he said. For this study, we want to know what Paul *meant* and how his audience *understood* him. Although we may not always be able to determine Paul's specific intent, that is our goal.

Interpretation implies understanding. Original meaning and context are important. Be reasonable. Compare.

Seek correct answers, but give yourself grace. A child's rendering of a ladybug on a blade of grass will not compare to Van Gogh's renderings, and yet, there is something wholly precious about the works of a child. Our renderings of Scripture won't ever equate to a Bible scholar's commentary. That's not our goal here. Our goal is knowing God. Sometimes this involves baby steps.

A, B, & C: TOOLS FOR INTERPRETATION

If the answers are not intuitive or easily found within the passage, tools are available to help us better understand. Our daily lesson format provides three boxes intended to support interpretation. Here, you'll find space to identify key words, define those key words, and record supporting verses (cross references). These are intended to help and guide you as you interpret Scripture. Use them however you find them to be helpful.

A. KEY WORDS: Did you notice that a word was repeated, seems important, is unfamiliar, or is interesting in any way? Record it here.

B. DEFINITIONS: Use this box to record definitions of the key words you listed. For definitions, we have options:

• *Read the verse using a different translation or version of the Bible.* This can be a very simple way to define a word. For example, our practice lesson (on page 22) notes the word **apostle** from I Timothy 1:1. The ESV translation says "apostle," while the Amplified Bible expounds: "apostle (special messenger, personally chosen representative)." [1]

• *Use a Bible concordance.* My favorite way to define a word is to use a concordance. This tool looks at words in their original language. I like the **Strong's Concordance**, which can also be found online.

i. Going online? Try **Blue Letter Bible**, a free web-based concordance.

ii. Once there, (referring to our practice lesson on page 22) simply type "I Timothy 1" into the "Search the Bible" box. Click on the box

---

[1] The Holy Bible: The Amplified Bible. 1987. La Habra, CA: The Lockman Foundation.

called **TOOLS** next to I Timothy 1:1 and an assortment of choices will arrive. Find the corresponding Strong's Concordance number for "apostle" (in this case: G652) and click on it. You'll retrieve the Greek word, original definitions, and how it is used in other places of the Bible. It's fascinating! Make note of the definitions you find.

• *Try a Bible dictionary.* In order to define people or find places, Bible dictionaries are handy.

i. Online, you can try **Bible Gateway, Blue Letter Bible,** or **Bible Hub** for free.

ii. There are also wonderful apps available for you to use. A friend recently introduced me to **Bible Map**. This app is simple to use and automatically syncs Scripture with maps.

C. CROSS REFERENCES: Some Bibles offer cross references. This is a solid way to allow Scripture to interpret Scripture. Perhaps your Bible does not include cross references (most journaling Bibles do not). No worries! It's very easy to access cross references online. **Bible Hub** is a great place to start!

Your daily lesson framework also offers space for you to identify the main point of the passage you've read. Here, you may summarize the main point(s) or any recurring themes you noticed in the passage. Understanding the main idea always helps us to interpret a scenario correctly.

WANTING EVEN MORE? Our daily study format includes space for key words, definitions, and cross references, along with space to identify the main points of the passage you're studying. However, there are other helps available if you'd like to dig deeper. Biblical commentaries are books written by Biblical scholars. Commentaries often provide solid cultural and historical context while commenting verse-by-verse on Scripture.

Personally, I admire the dedication and genius of the scholars who write commentaries. These amazingly dedicated scholars study for the glory of God. And yet, it's best to save these resources for last. Why? Because commentaries are not a substitute for reading and understanding God's Word on your own. Seek to understand on your own first.

Also, please note that commentaries are often written according to various theological bents. It's helpful to compare. Know your sources. This is especially crucial if roaming the Internet. Please surf with discernment and great care.

Still not satisfied? Note your question and talk to God about it. Ponder. Many times, as you ponder a verse, God will interpret. Other times, He allows certain things to remain a mystery. He is sovereign. We walk by faith.

Remember to share and discuss your questions with others at Bible study, either in person or online. Studying God's Word is meant to be done in community. We encourage, learn, and grow together.

Finally, check out our website: **www.simplybible.study**.

STEP 4: APPLICATION | *Put it all **together**.*

With the Holy Spirit's illumination, careful observation, and good interpretation, we better understand the meaning of a passage. And that's thrilling! Oftentimes, finding a nugget of truth, a promise, or a revelation about God Himself takes my breath away! There is no other book like it:

> For the word of God is living and active, sharper than any two-edged sword, piercing to the division of soul and of spirit, of joints and of marrow, and discerning the thoughts and intentions of the heart.
> *Hebrews 4:12*

The God of the Universe loves us and personally reveals Himself through His Living Word. When He does, it cuts in a good way. Then we're ready to *apply* His Word to our everyday lives.

Application is the fun and creative part. Yes, the original author of Scripture had one meaning, but the personal applications of Scripture are many. This part is between you and God. A particular verse, word, or idea might strike a chord in your heart. Slow down. Take note. Show God the discovery. This is the amazing process of God revealing Himself and His truth to you through His Word and the power of His Holy Spirit.

God looks at our hearts. He sees, knows, and loves His sheep. And so, He may use His Word to teach, correct, rebuke, or train. He is always equipping. (II Timothy 3:16-17) If you're willing, He will lead you to apply His Word specifically to your everyday life.

Application ideas include:
1. Worship God for who He is, according to a truth or promised discovered.
2. Thank Him for a lesson learned.
3. Note an example to follow.
4. Confess a sin revealed.
5. Pray a prayer noticed.
6. Obey, trust, and follow God's way, His command, His plan.
7. Memorize a verse.

WRAPPING UP: PRAYER | *Respond to a **holy God**.*

Application implies a recognition of who God is. And so, wrapping up personal study with application nearly always leads me to bow down in worship, at least bowing my heart. Hence, the **SIMPLY BIBLE** daily format includes a place for *prayer*. Please use this! It may be the most important space of all.

Enjoy being together with Him in His Word. Savor. Learn. Grow. Know. Thank. Praise. Love. Then carry a nugget of truth in your heart to ponder with Him as you go about your day.

lesson *samples*

PRACTICE LESSONS & EXAMPLES

practice *lesson*

A STEP-BY-STEP GUIDE

Below are two verses, I Timothy 1:1-2. As you read, feel free to highlight, circle, underline and mark up the text in whatever way you like. In the *Observe* column, jot down details that pop out and write down questions that come to mind. Then interpret. Simply use the Scripture itself or hop over to boxes A, B, and C to define a word or find a cross reference that will help you better understand.

Finish by summarizing, applying, and praying.

This is *your* workbook. It is meant to be a journal of your thoughts as you engage with God and His Word. Don't be shy. Be you, be with God, and enjoy!

READ	OBSERVE	INTERPRET
¹ Paul, an apostle of Christ Jesus by command of God our Savior and of Christ Jesus our hope, ² To Timothy, my true child in the faith: Grace, mercy, and peace from God the Father and Christ Jesus our Lord.		

KEY WORDS	DEFINITIONS	CROSS REFERENCES

MAIN POINT(S)

APPLY

PRAY

sample *lesson*

1 TIMOTHY 1:1-2 | FOR THOSE CRAZY, BUSY DAYS

Life gets hectic. We get busy. It happens. Some days, you just don't have the time to go very deep in your study. That's okay! But even reading just a few verses and aiming to hone in on *one* important detail is better than nothing at all! Here's what it might look like to observe, interpret, and apply just *one* thing:

READ	OBSERVE	INTERPRET
[1] Paul, an apostle of Christ Jesus by command of God our Savior and of Christ Jesus our hope, [2] To Timothy, my true child in the faith: Grace, mercy, and peace from God the Father and Christ Jesus our Lord.	Christ Jesus is mentioned 3 times. According to Paul, who is he?	Jesus is "our hope." He is "our Lord." He commanded Paul to be His apostle. He gives grace, mercy, and peace.

KEY WORDS	DEFINITIONS	CROSS REFERENCES
apostle	a special messenger, a personally-chosen representative (Amplified Bible)	**I Timothy 1:12** I thank him who has given me strength, Christ Jesus our Lord, because he judged me faithful, appointing me to his service...

MAIN POINT(S)

The apostle Paul greets Timothy in a letter.

APPLY

Even in a greeting of a letter, Paul brings glory to Jesus and reminds Timothy of the hope we have in Him. How can I greet others with this same exuberance for Christ throughout my day today?

PRAY

Lord God, thank You for today's reminder of hope. I praise You, Jesus, for **you are Lord.** And You are the giver of grace, mercy, and peace. Thank You! Like Paul, may I be a vessel of Your hope, grace, mercy, and peace today.

sample *lesson*

1 TIMOTHY 1:1-2 | GOING DEEPER

On occasion, you may find yourself wanting to go a little deeper in your study. Here's an example of what that could look like. You can observe as much or as little as you like. Remember: no two journals will look the same.

READ	OBSERVE	INTERPRET
[1] Paul, an apostle of Christ Jesus by command of God our Savior and of Christ Jesus our hope, [2] To Timothy, my true child in the faith: Grace, mercy, and peace from God the Father and Christ Jesus our Lord.	Who is Paul? What is an apostle? Christ Jesus is mentioned 3 times in two verses! Who is He? Why is He our hope? Who is Timothy? Paul refers to Timothy as "my" true child. Why? Faith in what? Is it common to offer grace, mercy, and peace in a greeting? Notice Paul distinguishes between God the Father and Jesus Christ.	Paul: an apostle of Jesus. Apostle: chosen by God Jesus is our hope and our Lord. He commanded Paul to be His apostle. He gives grace, mercy, and peace. Christ is our Savior. He is also "in us." (Col.1:27) Timothy: Paul's "true child in the faith." Not sure why Paul uses this phrase. Perhaps Paul witnessed to Timothy and was a part of his spiritual "birth." Faith: Belief in Christ. Mercy is found in other greetings: II Timothy 1, 2 John 3, Jude 2, but overall is unique for Paul to include in his letters.

KEY WORDS	DEFINITIONS	CROSS REFERENCES
apostle	a special messenger, a personally-chosen representative (Amplified Bible)	**I Timothy 1:12** - I thank him who has given me strength, Christ Jesus our Lord, because he judged me faithful, appointing me to his service...
hope	an expectation	**Colossians 1:27** - To them God chose to make known how great among the Gentiles are the riches of the glory of this mystery, which is Christ in you, the hope of glory.
true child in the faith		**Titus 1:4** - To Titus, my true child in a common faith...

MAIN POINT(S)

The apostle Paul greets Timothy in a letter.

APPLY

Even in a greeting, Paul brings glory to Jesus and reminds Timothy of the hope we have in Him. How can I greet others with this same exuberance for Christ? What am I doing to "give birth" to children of the faith? Praise God for His grace, peace, and mercy! Am I extending this to others?

PRAY

Lord God, thank You for today's reminder of hope. I praise You, Jesus, for **you are Lord.** And You are the giver of grace, mercy, and peace. Thank You! Like Paul, may I be a vessel of Your hope, grace, mercy, and peace today. Lord, I pray for open doors to share Christ with _____. Please prepare her heart to receive your grace and peace.

YOU DID IT! That's it. That's all there is to it. If this is your first time, perhaps the process felt awkward. Don't worry. You probably don't remember how clumsy and time-consuming it was the very first time you tried tying your shoe, riding a bike, or driving a car. Practice helps. Same for Bible study.

You're more observant, smarter, and stronger than you think you are. God created you that way. More importantly, He is with you. His desire is to be known. Lean into Him. Ask, seek, and you will find. His grace is sufficient. His power is made perfect in our weakness.

> For as the rain and the snow come down from heaven
>   and do not return there but water the earth,
> making it bring forth and sprout,
>   giving seed to the sower and bread to the eater,
> so shall my word be that goes out from my mouth;
>   it shall not return to me empty,
> but it shall accomplish that which I purpose,
>   and shall succeed in the thing for which I sent it.
> For you shall go out in joy
>   and be led forth in peace;
> the mountains and the hills before you
>   shall break forth into singing,
>   and all the trees of the field shall clap their hands.
>
> *Isaiah 55:10-12*

Lord God Almighty, thank You for Your Word! Like rain and snow watering the earth so that it might bud and flourish, may Your Word now water our hearts, minds, and souls to flourish in our love for You and for one another. May Your purposes and desires be accomplished. As we study with You, may we go out in joy and be led forth in Your peace. With all creation may we sing and clap for joy and bring glory to Your Name...

in *context*

EXAMINING THE CONTEXT OF GALATIANS

in *context*

EXAMINING THE CONTEXT OF GALATIANS

GALATIANS: A letter written by Paul to the churches in the Roman province of Galatia, a destination of Paul's missionary tours to the Gentiles. Cities of Galatia included Antioch, Lystra, Iconium, and Derbe.

Having initially received Paul's gospel message of Christ Jesus, the Galatians have now fallen prey to an opponent's "gospel" of false teaching known as "Judaizing." Judaizers sought to impose facets of Jewish law upon the believers including circumcision and diet restrictions. Paul is ready to rumble for the sake of their freedom. He even accuses Peter of succumbing to such false teaching. Throughout his letter, Paul contrasts the liberty of life "in Christ" versus the bondage of his opponent's "gospel."

According to ancient letter-writing handbooks, some scholars define Galatians as a "rebuke letter." Omitting an opening thanksgiving, this type of letter was sent to someone of close relationship who failed to follow instructions or who foolishly changed his mind. Exercising rhetorical persuasion, Paul censures and calls for the Galatians to consider the bondage of the law and return to the freedom found in his gospel of justification by faith in Christ alone.

Paul begins his persuasive argument by first explaining his own transformation from a life in Judaism to his new life in Christ. Therefore, to better understand his conversion, our study begins with a peek into Acts before actually digging into Galatians.

For further study, you may also enjoy reading Luke's account of the Jerusalem council as recorded in Acts 15. Here, the apostles and elders gathered to discuss whether or not Gentile believers were required to be circumcised. In the end, their decision backs up Paul's belief that Gentiles ought to be fully received into the family of God.

Themes of grace, freedom, and life in the Spirit abound. These are worth the rumble!

the roman *empire*

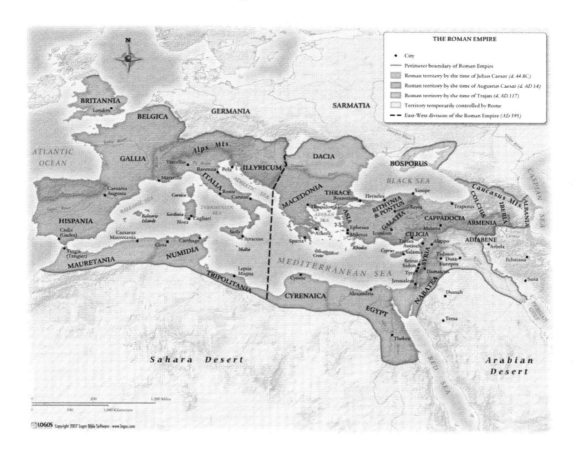

---

[1] Map provided by Logos Bible Software.

keeping *time*

A TIMELINE OF PAUL'S JOURNEY

28 — Jesus' public ministry begins (28-30)

30 — Jesus' crucifixion

32 —
  Paul's conversion

34 —
  Paul's first post-conversion Jerusalem visit

36 — Paul in Cilicia and Syria (35-46)

38 —

40 —

42 —

44 —

46 — Paul's second Jerusalem visit
  Paul and Barnabus in Cyprus and Galatia

48 — *Paul writes his letter to the Galatians (?)*
  Council of Jerusalem

50 — Paul & Silas travel from Syrian Antioch to Macedonia and Achaia (49-50)
  Paul writes his letter to the Thessalonians

52 — Paul in Corinth (50-52); Paul's third Jerusalem visit
  Paul in Ephesus (52-55)

54 —
  Paul writes his letters to the Corinthians (55-56)

56 — Paul in Macedonia, Illyricum, and Achaia
  Paul writes his letter to the Romans; Paul's final Jerusalem visit

58 — Paul's imprisonment in Caesarea (57-59)
  Paul's voyage to Rome begins

60 — Paul arrives in Rome
  Paul placed under house-arrest in Rome (60-62)

62 — *Paul writes his "captivity letters" (60-62?)*

64 —

---

[1] Bruce, F. F. (2000). *Paul, Apostle of the Heart Set Free.* Cumbria, UK: Paternoster Press.

compare and *contrast*

UNDER THE LAW VS. FREEDOM IN CHRIST

In Paul's letter to the Galatians, he often compares the differences between *relating to God through the law* versus *relating to God through Christ*, which is the gospel message he preached. Use this chart to keep record of the differences you find.

REFERENCE	LAW	CHRIST

compare and *contrast*

UNDER THE LAW VS. FREEDOM IN CHRIST

REFERENCE	LAW	CHRIST

the fruit of the *spirit*

BECOMING A **DOER** OF THE WORD

the fruit of the spirit *challenge*

BECOMING A **DOER** OF THE WORD

Do you want to be more mindful of the attributes of Christ's fruit? Are you praying for more evidence of love, joy, peace, patience, kindness, goodness, faithfulness, gentleness, or self-control in your life? Complete the "fruit of the spirit challenge" during this **SIMPLY BIBLE** study and watch as God continues His good work in you!

Each week throughout our study, choose to focus on one characteristic of God's fruit. Begin by *defining* it. You might even jot down a few notes for yourself on how God Himself displays the attribute you've chosen! Then, find practical ways to ponder and practice *living* it. Record one thought or action per day related to bearing this aspect of the Spirit's fruit.

WEEK One	FRUIT - *Faithfulness*
DEFINE - Not turning away, Keeping your word, being loyal and trustworthy, Walking with God and loved ones through every season	
SUNDAY	
MONDAY	
TUESDAY	
WEDNESDAY	
THURSDAY	
FRIDAY	I need to let my ego step aside.
SATURDAY	

WEEK	FRUIT
DEFINE	

SUNDAY	
MONDAY	
TUESDAY	
WEDNESDAY	
THURSDAY	
FRIDAY	
SATURDAY	

WEEK	FRUIT
DEFINE	

SUNDAY	
MONDAY	
TUESDAY	
WEDNESDAY	
THURSDAY	
FRIDAY	
SATURDAY	

WEEK	FRUIT
DEFINE	

SUNDAY	
MONDAY	
TUESDAY	
WEDNESDAY	
THURSDAY	
FRIDAY	
SATURDAY	

WEEK	FRUIT
DEFINE	

SUNDAY	
MONDAY	
TUESDAY	
WEDNESDAY	
THURSDAY	
FRIDAY	
SATURDAY	

WEEK	FRUIT
DEFINE	

SUNDAY	
MONDAY	
TUESDAY	
WEDNESDAY	
THURSDAY	
FRIDAY	
SATURDAY	

WEEK	FRUIT
DEFINE	

SUNDAY	
MONDAY	
TUESDAY	
WEDNESDAY	
THURSDAY	
FRIDAY	
SATURDAY	

FOR THROUGH THE SPIRIT,
BY FAITH, WE OURSELVES
EAGERLY WAIT FOR THE
HOPE OF RIGHTEOUSNESS.

GALATIANS 5:5

meet *paul*

PAUL'S EARLY LIFE & CONVERSION

take *note*

NOTES ON PAUL'S EARLY LIFE & CONVERSION

take *note*

NOTES ON PAUL'S EARLY LIFE & CONVERSION

day *one*

READ	OBSERVE	INTERPRET
[54] Now when they heard these things they were enraged, and they ground their teeth at him. [55] But he, full of the Holy Spirit, gazed into heaven and saw the glory of God, and Jesus standing at the right hand of God. [56] And he said, "Behold, I see the heavens opened, and the Son of Man standing at the right hand of God." [57] But they cried out with a loud voice and stopped their ears and rushed together at him. [58] Then they cast him out of the city and stoned him. And the witnesses laid down their garments at the feet of a young man named Saul. [59] And as they were stoning Stephen, he called out, "Lord Jesus, receive my spirit." [60] And falling to his knees he cried out with a loud voice, "Lord, do not hold this sin against them." And when he had said this, he fell asleep.	This is BEFORE Saul becomes Paul, which is important to note. Stephen surely was faithful and humble to the end "do not hold this sin against them" ↳ and we know	
[1] And Saul approved of his execution.		
And there arose on that day a great persecution against the church in Jerusalem, and they were all scattered throughout the regions of Judea and Samaria, except the apostles. [2] Devout men buried Stephen and made great lamentation over him. [3] But Saul was ravaging the church, and entering house after house, he dragged off men and women and committed them to prison.		

KEY WORDS	DEFINITIONS	CROSS REFERENCES

MAIN POINT(S)

APPLY

PRAY

day *two*

ACTS 9:1-9

READ	OBSERVE	INTERPRET
¹ But Saul, still breathing threats and murder against the disciples of the Lord, went to the high priest ² and asked him for letters to the synagogues at Damascus, so that if he found any belonging to the Way, men or women, he might bring them bound to Jerusalem. ³ Now as he went on his way, he approached Damascus, and suddenly a light from heaven shone around him. ⁴ And falling to the ground, he heard a voice saying to him, "Saul, Saul, why are you persecuting me?" ⁵ And he said, "Who are you, Lord?" And he said, "I am Jesus, whom you are persecuting. ⁶ But rise and enter the city, and you will be told what you are to do." ⁷ The men who were traveling with him stood speechless, hearing the voice but seeing no one. ⁸ Saul rose from the ground, and although his eyes were opened, he saw nothing. So they led him by the hand and brought him into Damascus. ⁹ And for three days he was without sight, and neither ate nor drank.		

KEY WORDS	DEFINITIONS	CROSS REFERENCES

MAIN POINT(S)

APPLY

PRAY

day *three*

ACTS 9:10-19

READ	OBSERVE	INTERPRET
[10] Now there was a disciple at Damascus named Ananias. The Lord said to him in a vision, "Ananias." And he said, "Here I am, Lord." [11] And the Lord said to him, "Rise and go to the street called Straight, and at the house of Judas look for a man of Tarsus named Saul, for behold, he is praying, [12] and he has seen in a vision a man named Ananias come in and lay his hands on him so that he might regain his sight." [13] But Ananias answered, "Lord, I have heard from many about this man, how much evil he has done to your saints at Jerusalem. [14] And here he has authority from the chief priests to bind all who call on your name." [15] But the Lord said to him, "Go, for he is a chosen instrument of mine to carry my name before the Gentiles and kings and the children of Israel. [16] For I will show him how much he must suffer for the sake of my name." [17] So Ananias departed and entered the house. And laying his hands on him he said, "Brother Saul, the Lord Jesus who appeared to you on the road by which you came has sent me so that you may regain your sight and be filled with the Holy Spirit." [18] And immediately something like scales fell from his eyes, and he regained his sight. Then he rose and was baptized; [19] and taking food, he was strengthened.		

KEY WORDS	DEFINITIONS	CROSS REFERENCES

MAIN POINT(S)

APPLY

PRAY

day *four*

READ

For some days he was with the disciples at Damascus. ²⁰ And immediately he proclaimed Jesus in the synagogues, saying, "He is the Son of God." ²¹ And all who heard him were amazed and said, "Is not this the man who made havoc in Jerusalem of those who called upon this name? And has he not come here for this purpose, to bring them bound before the chief priests?" ²² But Saul increased all the more in strength, and confounded the Jews who lived in Damascus by proving that Jesus was the Christ.

²³ When many days had passed, the Jews plotted to kill him, ²⁴ but their plot became known to Saul. They were watching the gates day and night in order to kill him, ²⁵ but his disciples took him by night and let him down through an opening in the wall, lowering him in a basket.

²⁶ And when he had come to Jerusalem, he attempted to join the disciples. And they were all afraid of him, for they did not believe that he was a disciple. ²⁷ But Barnabas took him and brought him to the apostles and declared to them how on the road he had seen the Lord, who spoke to him, and how at Damascus he had preached boldly in the name of Jesus. ²⁸ So he went in and out among them at Jerusalem, preaching boldly in the name of the Lord. ²⁹ And he spoke and disputed against the Hellenists. But they were seeking to kill him. ³⁰ And when the brothers learned this, they brought him down to Caesarea and sent him off to Tarsus.

OBSERVE

INTERPRET

KEY WORDS	DEFINITIONS	CROSS REFERENCES

MAIN POINT(S)

APPLY

PRAY

day *five*

1 Summary:	2 Write out (or rewrite in your own words) your favorite verse from this week's readings.
3 How is Paul introduced? Describe Paul's role and persecution against the church (7:54-8:3).	4 How does Stephen's death and prayer remind you of Christ? Could you pray this for your own "enemies?" Why or why not?
5 Where is Paul headed in Acts 9:1-2? Why?	6 Who does Paul encounter in Acts 9:1-9? Describe how he is changed.

7 Have you ever maintained a wrong view of God? What circumstances led you to change your outlook?

8 In Acts 9:10-19, Ananias encounters the Lord. What do you admire in Ananias?

9 List all that Paul receives in Acts 9:17-19.

10 Re-read Acts 9:19-25. Rather than persecuting Christ followers, what does Paul do in Damascus? What is most remarkable to you?

Commit to pray for one unbeliever who seems unlikely to believe in Christ.

11 How is Paul received in Jerusalem? What role does Barnabas play? What can we learn from him?

12 Praise God for at least one truth from this week's study:

take it to *heart*

USE THIS SPACE TO WRITE OUT OR JOURNAL A FAVORITE
VERSE OR PASSAGE FROM THIS WEEK'S STUDY

...FOR HE IS A CHOSEN
INSTRUMENT OF MINE
TO CARRY MY NAME
BEFORE THE GENTILES
AND KINGS AND THE
CHILDREN OF ISRAEL.

ACTS 9:15

chapter *one*

GALATIANS

take *note*

NOTES ON GALATIANS 1

take *note*

day *one*

GALATIANS 1:1-5

READ	OBSERVE	INTERPRET
[1] Paul, an apostle—not from men nor through man, but through Jesus Christ and God the Father, who raised him from the dead— [2] and all the brothers who are with me, To the churches of Galatia: [3] Grace to you and peace from God our Father and the Lord Jesus Christ, [4] who gave himself for our sins to deliver us from the present evil age, according to the will of our God and Father, [5] to whom be the glory forever and ever. Amen.		

KEY WORDS	DEFINITIONS	CROSS REFERENCES

MAIN POINT(S)

APPLY

PRAY

day *two*

GALATIANS 1:6-9

READ	OBSERVE	INTERPRET
⁶ I am astonished that you are so quickly deserting him who called you in the grace of Christ and are turning to a different gospel— ⁷ not that there is another one, but there are some who trouble you and want to distort the gospel of Christ. ⁸ But even if we or an angel from heaven should preach to you a gospel contrary to the one we preached to you, let him be accursed. ⁹ As we have said before, so now I say again: If anyone is preaching to you a gospel contrary to the one you received, let him be accursed.		

KEY WORDS	DEFINITIONS	CROSS REFERENCES

MAIN POINT(S)

APPLY

PRAY

day *three*

GALATIANS 1:10-12

READ	OBSERVE	INTERPRET
¹⁰ For am I now seeking the approval of man, or of God? Or am I trying to please man? If I were still trying to please man, I would not be a servant of Christ. ¹¹ For I would have you know, brothers, that the gospel that was preached by me is not man's gospel. ¹² For I did not receive it from any man, nor was I taught it, but I received it through a revelation of Jesus Christ.		

KEY WORDS	DEFINITIONS	CROSS REFERENCES

MAIN POINT(S)

APPLY

PRAY

day *four*

READ	OBSERVE	INTERPRET
¹³ For you have heard of my former life in Judaism, how I persecuted the church of God violently and tried to destroy it. ¹⁴ And I was advancing in Judaism beyond many of my own age among my people, so extremely zealous was I for the traditions of my fathers. ¹⁵ But when he who had set me apart before I was born, and who called me by his grace, ¹⁶ was pleased to reveal his Son to me, in order that I might preach him among the Gentiles, I did not immediately consult with anyone; ¹⁷ nor did I go up to Jerusalem to those who were apostles before me, but I went away into Arabia, and returned again to Damascus.		
¹⁸ Then after three years I went up to Jerusalem to visit Cephas and remained with him fifteen days. ¹⁹ But I saw none of the other apostles except James the Lord's brother. ²⁰ (In what I am writing to you, before God, I do not lie!) ²¹ Then I went into the regions of Syria and Cilicia. ²² And I was still unknown in person to the churches of Judea that are in Christ. ²³ They only were hearing it said, "He who used to persecute us is now preaching the faith he once tried to destroy." ²⁴ And they glorified God because of me.		

KEY WORDS	DEFINITIONS	CROSS REFERENCES

MAIN POINT(S)

APPLY

PRAY

day *five*

GALATIANS 1 | REVIEW & DISCUSSION QUESTIONS

1 Summary:	2 Write out a favorite verse(s) from the passage, perhaps in your own words:
3 In verse 1, Paul refers to himself as an apostle. Define *apostle*. How does Paul explain his own apostleship (1:11-12)? How does *apostle* differ from *disciple*?	4 According to Galatians 1:1-5, how would you define the "gospel of Christ" according to Paul?
5 Paul seems upset. Why is Paul writing to the Galatians?	6 What is Judaism (1:13)? How does Judaism differ from the gospel of Christ?

7 What does Paul say concerning those who pervert the gospel (1:9)? Why is this a big deal?

8 In what ways are you personally tempted to add to the gospel of Christ?

9 **True or false:** *Paul seeks to please men.* Share a time when your own testimony was affected by "people pleasing."

10 Compare and contrast Paul before and after his conversion.

11 Share your own conversion story. How are you different after receiving and believing Christ?

12 Praise God for at least one truth from this week's study:

take it to *heart*

FOR AM I NOW SEEKING
THE APPROVAL OF MAN,
OR OF GOD?

GALATIANS 1:10

chapter *two*

GALATIANS

take *note*

NOTES ON GALATIANS 2

take *note*

NOTES ON GALATIANS 2

day *one*

GALATIANS 2:1-5

READ	OBSERVE	INTERPRET
[1] Then after fourteen years I went up again to Jerusalem with Barnabas, taking Titus along with me. [2] I went up because of a revelation and set before them (though privately before those who seemed influential) the gospel that I proclaim among the Gentiles, in order to make sure I was not running or had not run in vain. [3] But even Titus, who was with me, was not forced to be circumcised, though he was a Greek. [4] Yet because of false brothers secretly brought in—who slipped in to spy out our freedom that we have in Christ Jesus, so that they might bring us into slavery— [5] to them we did not yield in submission even for a moment, so that the truth of the gospel might be preserved for you.		

KEY WORDS	DEFINITIONS	CROSS REFERENCES

MAIN POINT(S)

APPLY

PRAY

day *two*

GALATIANS 2:6-10

READ	OBSERVE	INTERPRET
[6] And from those who seemed to be influential (what they were makes no difference to me; God shows no partiality)-those, I say, who seemed influential added nothing to me. [7] On the contrary, when they saw that I had been entrusted with the gospel to the uncircumcised, just as Peter had been entrusted with the gospel to the circumcised [8] (for he who worked through Peter for his apostolic ministry to the circumcised worked also through me for mine to the Gentiles), [9] and when James and Cephas and John, who seemed to be pillars, perceived the grace that was given to me, they gave the right hand of fellowship to Barnabas and me, that we should go to the Gentiles and they to the circumcised. [10] Only, they asked us to remember the poor, the very thing I was eager to do.		

KEY WORDS	DEFINITIONS	CROSS REFERENCES

MAIN POINT(S)

APPLY

PRAY

day *three*

READ	OBSERVE	INTERPRET
[11] But when Cephas came to Antioch, I opposed him to his face, because he stood condemned. [12] For before certain men came from James, he was eating with the Gentiles; but when they came he drew back and separated himself, fearing the circumcision party. [13] And the rest of the Jews acted hypocritically along with him, so that even Barnabas was led astray by their hypocrisy. [14] But when I saw that their conduct was not in step with the truth of the gospel, I said to Cephas before them all, "If you, though a Jew, live like a Gentile and not like a Jew, how can you force the Gentiles to live like Jews?"		

KEY WORDS	DEFINITIONS	CROSS REFERENCES

MAIN POINT(S)

APPLY

PRAY

day *four*

READ	OBSERVE	INTERPRET
[15] We ourselves are Jews by birth and not Gentile sinners; [16] yet we know that a person is not justified by works of the law but through faith in Jesus Christ, so we also have believed in Christ Jesus, in order to be justified by faith in Christ and not by works of the law, because by works of the law no one will be justified. [17] But if, in our endeavor to be justified in Christ, we too were found to be sinners, is Christ then a servant of sin? Certainly not! [18] For if I rebuild what I tore down, I prove myself to be a transgressor. [19] For through the law I died to the law, so that I might live to God. [20] I have been crucified with Christ. It is no longer I who live, but Christ who lives in me. And the life I now live in the flesh I live by faith in the Son of God, who loved me and gave himself for me. [21] I do not nullify the grace of God, for if righteousness were through the law, then Christ died for no purpose.		

KEY WORDS	DEFINITIONS	CROSS REFERENCES

MAIN POINT(S)

APPLY

PRAY

day *five*

GALATIANS 2 | REVIEW & DISCUSSION QUESTIONS

1 Summary:	2 Write out a favorite verse(s) from the passage, perhaps in your own words:
3 At this time, why did Paul go to Jerusalem (2:1-2)? For more info, see Acts 15:1-11.	4 Who did Paul take with him to Jerusalem and why is this important (2:3)?
5 Verse 10 shows a high priority by the apostles for service to whom? On a scale of 1-10, how well are you doing at this? *Commit to pray about a specific step you can take this week.*	6 What was Peter's mistake (2:11-13)? What do you think led to it?

7 As a Christ follower, "fear of what others think" can affect actions. How have you experienced this fear? How do we overcome it?

8 Define "justification by faith" (2:14-16).

9 In verse 20, what does Paul mean by, "I have been crucified with Christ?"

10 Explain the difference between following the law (being a good, moral person) and being a Christian.

11 Do you ever feel insecure in your relationship with Christ? What might this tell you?

12 Praise God for at least one truth from this week's study:

take it to *heart*

USE THIS SPACE TO WRITE OUT OR JOURNAL A FAVORITE
VERSE OR PASSAGE FROM THIS WEEK'S STUDY

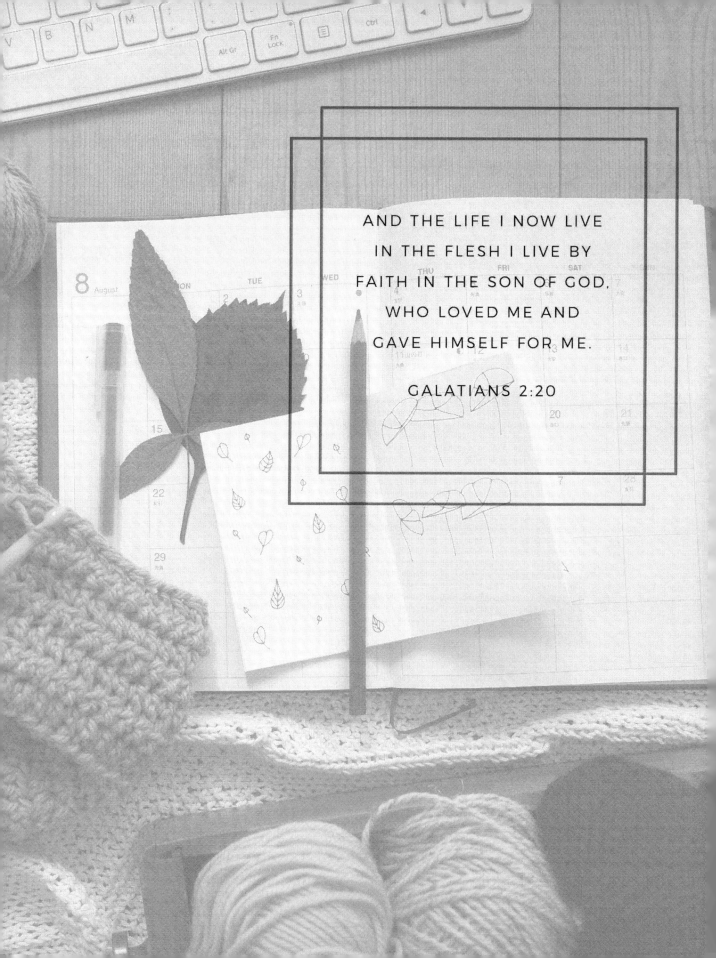

AND THE LIFE I NOW LIVE
IN THE FLESH I LIVE BY
FAITH IN THE SON OF GOD,
WHO LOVED ME AND
GAVE HIMSELF FOR ME.

GALATIANS 2:20

chapter *three*

GALATIANS

take *note*

NOTES ON GALATIANS 3

take *note*

NOTES ON GALATIANS 3

---

day *one*

READ	OBSERVE	INTERPRET
[1] O foolish Galatians! Who has bewitched you? It was before your eyes that Jesus Christ was publicly portrayed as crucified. [2] Let me ask you only this: Did you receive the Spirit by works of the law or by hearing with faith? [3] Are you so foolish? Having begun by the Spirit, are you now being perfected by the flesh? [4] Did you suffer so many things in vain—if indeed it was in vain? [5] Does he who supplies the Spirit to you and works miracles among you do so by works of the law, or by hearing with faith— [6] just as Abraham "believed God, and it was counted to him as righteousness"? [7] Know then that it is those of faith who are the sons of Abraham. [8] And the Scripture, foreseeing that God would justify the Gentiles by faith, preached the gospel beforehand to Abraham, saying, "In you shall all the nations be blessed." [9] So then, those who are of faith are blessed along with Abraham, the man of faith.		

KEY WORDS	DEFINITIONS	CROSS REFERENCES

MAIN POINT(S)

APPLY

PRAY

day *two*

READ	OBSERVE	INTERPRET
¹⁰ For all who rely on works of the law are under a curse; for it is written, "Cursed be everyone who does not abide by all things written in the Book of the Law, and do them." ¹¹ Now it is evident that no one is justified before God by the law, for "The righteous shall live by faith." ¹² But the law is not of faith, rather "The one who does them shall live by them." ¹³ Christ redeemed us from the curse of the law by becoming a curse for us—for it is written, "Cursed is everyone who is hanged on a tree"— ¹⁴ so that in Christ Jesus the blessing of Abraham might come to the Gentiles, so that we might receive the promised Spirit through faith.		

KEY WORDS	DEFINITIONS	CROSS REFERENCES

MAIN POINT(S)

APPLY

PRAY

day *three*

GALATIANS 3:15-18

READ	OBSERVE	INTERPRET
[15] To give a human example, brothers: even with a man-made covenant, no one annuls it or adds to it once it has been ratified. [16] Now the promises were made to Abraham and to his offspring. It does not say, "And to offsprings," referring to many, but referring to one, "And to your offspring," who is Christ. [17] This is what I mean: the law, which came 430 years afterward, does not annul a covenant previously ratified by God, so as to make the promise void. [18] For if the inheritance comes by the law, it no longer comes by promise; but God gave it to Abraham by a promise.		

KEY WORDS	DEFINITIONS	CROSS REFERENCES

MAIN POINT(S)

APPLY

PRAY

day *four*

READ	OBSERVE	INTERPRET
[19] Why then the law? It was added because of transgressions, until the offspring should come to whom the promise had been made, and it was put in place through angels by an intermediary. [20] Now an intermediary implies more than one, but God is one. [21] Is the law then contrary to the promises of God? Certainly not! For if a law had been given that could give life, then righteousness would indeed be by the law. [22] But the Scripture imprisoned everything under sin, so that the promise by faith in Jesus Christ might be given to those who believe. [23] Now before faith came, we were held captive under the law, imprisoned until the coming faith would be revealed. [24] So then, the law was our guardian until Christ came, in order that we might be justified by faith. [25] But now that faith has come, we are no longer under a guardian, [26] for in Christ Jesus you are all sons of God, through faith. [27] For as many of you as were baptized into Christ have put on Christ. [28] There is neither Jew nor Greek, there is neither slave nor free, there is no male and female, for you are all one in Christ Jesus. [29] And if you are Christ's, then you are Abraham's offspring, heirs according to promise.		

KEY WORDS	DEFINITIONS	CROSS REFERENCES

MAIN POINT(S)

APPLY

PRAY

day *five*

GALATIANS 3 | REVIEW & DISCUSSION QUESTIONS

1 Summary:	2 Write out a favorite verse(s) from the passage, perhaps in your own words:
3 Using verses 1-5, compare and contrast the law versus faith.	4 Why does Paul refer to the Galatians as "foolish?" How do you react to this? Is he too harsh? Why or why not?
5 Why is the law (legalism) sometimes appealing? Give an example of a church or Christian practice that is unnecessary. What is a necessary practice?	6 Consider and explain Abraham's righteousness (3:6-9; Genesis 15:1-6). How is this meaningful to you?

7 What is Paul's point in his discussion of the "curse of the law" (3:10-14)?

8 What was the purpose of the law (3:24-25)? Does it matter if I obey the law today? Why or why not?

9 Christ redeems us from the curse. What has he taken? What has he given?

10 In verses 26-27, what does it mean to "put on" Christ?

11 In your own words, explain verse 28.

12 Praise God for at least one truth from this week's study:

take it to *heart*

USE THIS SPACE TO WRITE OUT OR JOURNAL A FAVORITE
VERSE OR PASSAGE FROM THIS WEEK'S STUDY

...FOR IN CHRIST JESUS
YOU ARE ALL SONS OF
GOD, THROUGH FAITH.

GALATIANS 3:26

chapter *four*

GALATIANS

take *note*

NOTES ON GALATIANS 4

take *note*

NOTES ON GALATIANS 4

day *one*

GALATIANS 4:1-7

READ	OBSERVE	INTERPRET
[1] I mean that the heir, as long as he is a child, is no different from a slave, though he is the owner of everything, [2] but he is under guardians and managers until the date set by his father. [3] In the same way we also, when we were children, were enslaved to the elementary principles of the world. [4] But when the fullness of time had come, God sent forth his Son, born of woman, born under the law, [5] to redeem those who were under the law, so that we might receive adoption as sons. [6] And because you are sons, God has sent the Spirit of his Son into our hearts, crying, "Abba! Father!" [7] So you are no longer a slave, but a son, and if a son, then an heir through God.		

KEY WORDS	DEFINITIONS	CROSS REFERENCES

MAIN POINT(S)

APPLY

PRAY

day *two*

GALATIANS 4:8-11

READ	OBSERVE	INTERPRET
[8] Formerly, when you did not know God, you were enslaved to those that by nature are not gods. [9] But now that you have come to know God, or rather to be known by God, how can you turn back again to the weak and worthless elementary principles of the world, whose slaves you want to be once more? [10] You observe days and months and seasons and years! [11] I am afraid I may have labored over you in vain.		

KEY WORDS	DEFINITIONS	CROSS REFERENCES

MAIN POINT(S)

APPLY

PRAY

day *three*

GALATIANS 4:12-20

READ	OBSERVE	INTERPRET
[12] Brothers, I entreat you, become as I am, for I also have become as you are. You did me no wrong. [13] You know it was because of a bodily ailment that I preached the gospel to you at first, [14] and though my condition was a trial to you, you did not scorn or despise me, but received me as an angel of God, as Christ Jesus. [15] What then has become of your blessedness? For I testify to you that, if possible, you would have gouged out your eyes and given them to me. [16] Have I then become your enemy by telling you the truth? [17] They make much of you, but for no good purpose. They want to shut you out, that you may make much of them. [18] It is always good to be made much of for a good purpose, and not only when I am present with you, [19] my little children, for whom I am again in the anguish of childbirth until Christ is formed in you! [20] I wish I could be present with you now and change my tone, for I am perplexed about you.		

KEY WORDS	DEFINITIONS	CROSS REFERENCES

MAIN POINT(S)

APPLY

PRAY

day *four*

READ	OBSERVE	INTERPRET
21 Tell me, you who desire to be under the law, do you not listen to the law? 22 For it is written that Abraham had two sons, one by a slave woman and one by a free woman. 23 But the son of the slave was born according to the flesh, while the son of the free woman was born through promise. 24 Now this may be interpreted allegorically: these women are two covenants. One is from Mount Sinai, bearing children for slavery; she is Hagar. 25 Now Hagar is Mount Sinai in Arabia; she corresponds to the present Jerusalem, for she is in slavery with her children. 26 But the Jerusalem above is free, and she is our mother. 27 For it is written, "Rejoice, O barren one who does not bear; break forth and cry aloud, you who are not in labor! For the children of the desolate one will be more than those of the one who has a husband." 28 Now you, brothers, like Isaac, are children of promise. 29 But just as at that time he who was born according to the flesh persecuted him who was born according to the Spirit, so also it is now. 30 But what does the Scripture say? "Cast out the slave woman and her son, for the son of the slave woman shall not inherit with the son of the free woman." 31 So, brothers, we are not children of the slave but of the free woman.		

KEY WORDS	DEFINITIONS	CROSS REFERENCES

MAIN POINT(S)

APPLY

PRAY

day *five*

GALATIANS 4 | REVIEW & DISCUSSION QUESTIONS

1 Summary:	2 Write out a favorite verse(s) from the passage, perhaps in your own words:
3 Compare and contrast the child of God and the slave.	4 If your identity is grounded in being Christ's child, how might this practically apply to one area of your daily life and behavior? (Perhaps pinpoint a place where you have sought your identity apart from being God's child.)
5 According to verses 6-7, what is the importance of the Holy Spirit?	6 What is Paul's concern for the Galatians (4:8-11)?

7 What is his personal fear (4:11)? Have you ever experienced this same fear? Explain.

8 We often associate sin and enslavement. However, godly disciplines can also be enslaving. When are disciplines useful and when do they hold someone captive?

9 In verse 9, how do you explain the difference between knowing God and being known by God?

10 Explain how Paul's allegory between the slave and free woman connects to God's covenant and the Galatians (4:21-31).

11 In your own words, what is Paul telling the Galatians? How do you apply this to yourself?

12 Praise God for at least one truth from this week's study:

take it to *heart*

SO YOU ARE NO LONGER
A SLAVE, BUT A SON,
AND IF A SON, THEN AN
HEIR THROUGH GOD.

GALATIANS 4:7

chapter *five*

GALATIANS

take *note*

NOTES ON GALATIANS 5

take *note*

NOTES ON GALATIANS 5

day *one*

GALATIANS 5:1-6

READ	OBSERVE	INTERPRET
[1] For freedom Christ has set us free; stand firm therefore, and do not submit again to a yoke of slavery. [2] Look: I, Paul, say to you that if you accept circumcision, Christ will be of no advantage to you. [3] I testify again to every man who accepts circumcision that he is obligated to keep the whole law. [4] You are severed from Christ, you who would be justified by the law; you have fallen away from grace. [5] For through the Spirit, by faith, we ourselves eagerly wait for the hope of righteousness. [6] For in Christ Jesus neither circumcision nor uncircumcision counts for anything, but only faith working through love.		

KEY WORDS	DEFINITIONS	CROSS REFERENCES

MAIN POINT(S)

APPLY

PRAY

day *two*

READ	OBSERVE	INTERPRET
[7] You were running well. Who hindered you from obeying the truth? [8] This persuasion is not from him who calls you. [9] A little leaven leavens the whole lump. [10] I have confidence in the Lord that you will take no other view, and the one who is troubling you will bear the penalty, whoever he is. [11] But if I, brothers, still preach circumcision, why am I still being persecuted? In that case the offense of the cross has been removed. [12] I wish those who unsettle you would emasculate themselves! [13] For you were called to freedom, brothers. Only do not use your freedom as an opportunity for the flesh, but through love serve one another. [14] For the whole law is fulfilled in one word: "You shall love your neighbor as yourself." [15] But if you bite and devour one another, watch out that you are not consumed by one another.		

KEY WORDS

DEFINITIONS

CROSS REFERENCES

MAIN POINT(S)

APPLY

PRAY

day *three*

READ	OBSERVE	INTERPRET
[16] But I say, walk by the Spirit, and you will not gratify the desires of the flesh. [17] For the desires of the flesh are against the Spirit, and the desires of the Spirit are against the flesh, for these are opposed to each other, to keep you from doing the things you want to do. [18] But if you are led by the Spirit, you are not under the law. [19] Now the works of the flesh are evident: sexual immorality, impurity, sensuality, [20] idolatry, sorcery, enmity, strife, jealousy, fits of anger, rivalries, dissensions, divisions, [21] envy, drunkenness, orgies, and things like these. I warn you, as I warned you before, that those who do such things will not inherit the kingdom of God.		

KEY WORDS	DEFINITIONS	CROSS REFERENCES

MAIN POINT(S)

APPLY

PRAY

day *four*

READ	OBSERVE	INTERPRET
22 But the fruit of the Spirit is love, joy, peace, patience, kindness, goodness, faithfulness, 23 gentleness, self-control; against such things there is no law. 24 And those who belong to Christ Jesus have crucified the flesh with its passions and desires. 25 If we live by the Spirit, let us also keep in step with the Spirit. 26 Let us not become conceited, provoking one another, envying one another.		

KEY WORDS	DEFINITIONS	CROSS REFERENCES

MAIN POINT(S)

APPLY

PRAY

day *five*

GALATIANS 5 | REVIEW & DISCUSSION QUESTIONS

1 Summary:	2 Write out a favorite verse(s) from the passage, perhaps in your own words:
3 What is Paul's meaning in verse 1? In what ways do the Galatians need to stand firm? What will be the consequence of not standing firm?	4 In verse 6, what value does Paul give "the law?" Why? What is of value?
5 What is the purpose of leaven? Explain Paul's word picture for the church (5:9).	6 Explain "the offense of the cross" (5:11). How would circumcision abolish this offense?

7 Refer to verse 16. How do you walk by the Spirit? Practically, what does this look like?

8 Using Paul's list of sinful desires, what do you learn about yourself?

9 Considering the fruit of the Holy Spirit, what do you learn about God? Yourself?

10 Choose one aspect of the Spirit's fruit you desire and define it. Pray over it.

11 In daily life, are you more apt to live by rules and effort or by the power of the Spirit? Explain.

12 Praise God for at least one truth from this week's study:

take it to *heart*

USE THIS SPACE TO WRITE OUT OR JOURNAL A FAVORITE
VERSE OR PASSAGE FROM THIS WEEK'S STUDY

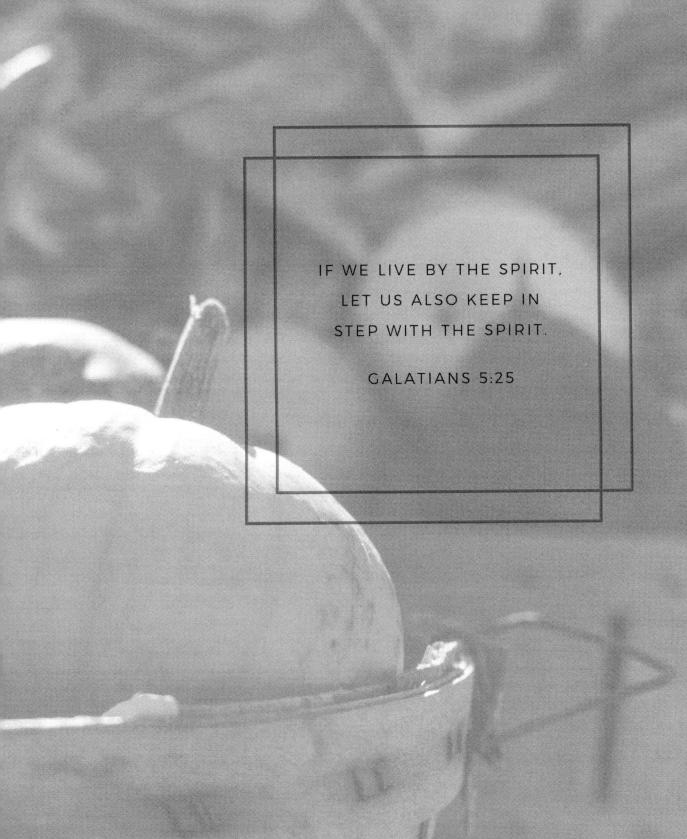

IF WE LIVE BY THE SPIRIT,
LET US ALSO KEEP IN
STEP WITH THE SPIRIT.

GALATIANS 5:25

chapter six

GALATIANS

take *note*

NOTES ON GALATIANS 6

take *note*

NOTES ON GALATIANS 6

day *one*

GALATIANS 6:1-5

READ	OBSERVE	INTERPRET
[1] Brothers, if anyone is caught in any transgression, you who are spiritual should restore him in a spirit of gentleness. Keep watch on yourself, lest you too be tempted. [2] Bear one another's burdens, and so fulfill the law of Christ. [3] For if anyone thinks he is something, when he is nothing, he deceives himself. [4] But let each one test his own work, and then his reason to boast will be in himself alone and not in his neighbor. [5] For each will have to bear his own load.		

KEY WORDS	DEFINITIONS	CROSS REFERENCES

MAIN POINT(S)

APPLY

PRAY

day *two*

READ	OBSERVE	INTERPRET
⁶ Let the one who is taught the word share all good things with the one who teaches. ⁷ Do not be deceived: God is not mocked, for whatever one sows, that will he also reap. ⁸ For the one who sows to his own flesh will from the flesh reap corruption, but the one who sows to the Spirit will from the Spirit reap eternal life. ⁹ And let us not grow weary of doing good, for in due season we will reap, if we do not give up. ¹⁰ So then, as we have opportunity, let us do good to everyone, and especially to those who are of the household of faith.		

KEY WORDS	DEFINITIONS	CROSS REFERENCES

MAIN POINT(S)

APPLY

PRAY

day *three*

GALATIANS 6:11-13

READ

For today's reading, please look up the passage in your own Bible and hand-write the verses here.

OBSERVE

INTERPRET

KEY WORDS	DEFINITIONS	CROSS REFERENCES

MAIN POINT(S)

APPLY

PRAY

day *four*

GALATIANS 6:14-18

READ

For today's reading, please look up the passage in your own Bible and hand-write the verses here.

OBSERVE

INTERPRET

KEY WORDS	DEFINITIONS	CROSS REFERENCES

MAIN POINT(S)

APPLY

PRAY

day *five*

GALATIANS 6 | REVIEW & DISCUSSION QUESTIONS

1 Summary:	2 Write out a favorite verse(s) from the passage, perhaps in your own words:
3 On a scale of 1-10, how easy is it to confront sin with gentleness (6:1)? Why is it often easier to overlook sin?	4 Provide an example of carrying another's burden. Who has helped you carry a burden? Grade yourself: how well are you doing at this?
5 Rarely do we begin a day looking to fall into sin. How do we "watch" ourselves in order to keep from sinning?	6 In verses 7-8, what does Paul mean concerning "reaping" what we sow?

7 Practically, what does it look like to sow in the flesh? The Spirit?

8 Considering Paul's words in verse 9, when are you most apt to grow weary of doing good? What helps you to persevere?

9 From verses 1-10, which exhortation of Paul's most tugs at your heart today? Why?

10 Beginning at verse 11, what does Paul personally do to end his letter? What main message is on his heart for the Galatians?

11 Ask God to reveal what you are boasting in apart from Christ's work. Confess. Remember: He has made you a new creation!

12 Praise God for at least one truth from this week's study:

take it to *heart*

USE THIS SPACE TO WRITE OUT OR JOURNAL A FAVORITE
VERSE OR PASSAGE FROM THIS WEEK'S STUDY

BEAR ONE ANOTHER'S
BURDENS, AND SO FULFILL
THE LAW OF CHRIST.

GALATIANS 6:2

final *thoughts*

WRAPPING UP

final *thoughts*

THE BOOK OF GALATIANS | WRAPPING UP

1 Choose your favorite verse from Galatians. Write it out here. Give an explanation of what this verse means to you or why you find it impactful.	2 Consider the book of Galatians as a whole. What overarching themes did you notice within this book throughout your study?
3 How would you summarize the book of Galatians in a single word?	4 Praise God for a truth that He has revealed to you or for a way that He has worked in your life as a result of your study of Galatians:

pause and *reflect*

USE THIS SPACE TO WRITE OUT A PRAYER, A KEY PASSAGE, OR A REFLECTION ON YOUR STUDY OF GALATIANS

I HAVE BEEN CRUCIFIED
WITH CHRIST. IT IS NO
LONGER I WHO LIVE, BUT
CHRIST WHO LIVES IN ME.

GALATIANS 2:20

leader *guide*

MAXIMIZING THE SMALL-GROUP EXPERIENCE

GO THEREFORE AND MAKE
DISCIPLES OF ALL NATIONS,
BAPTIZING THEM IN THE
NAME OF THE FATHER AND
OF THE SON AND OF THE
HOLY SPIRIT, TEACHING THEM
TO OBSERVE ALL THAT I
HAVE COMMANDED YOU.

MATTHEW 28:19-20

introduction

LEADING WOMEN THROUGH **SIMPLY BIBLE**

Welcome to **SIMPLY BIBLE**, and thank you for your commitment to walk alongside a group of women for this season of exploring God's Word. In my own life, God has proven Himself faithful. Time and again as I lead women and seek to be a blessing to others, the blessing always seems to be mine. He is gracious that way. So, it is my heartfelt prayer for leaders that, as you seek to be a blessing to others, you too will be blessed beyond measure by the experience of shepherding women through God's Word. Truly, what a privilege it is to facilitate conversations that point women to Christ!

The primary objective of **SIMPLY BIBLE** is this:

> To inspire every woman to love God with all her heart, soul, mind, and strength, and to love others as herself. (Luke 10:27)

And *you*, the small-group leader, will play an important role in inspiring women to do exactly that! You will lead your group through meaningful conversations, with the help of the discussion questions found at the end of every chapter in this workbook. Our intention here is to help women grow in their relationships with Jesus Christ. It is also my hope that you will connect with the women in your groups on a personal level, gently guiding them to authentic relationships with one another.

guarding your *heart*

LEADING FROM THE RIGHT PERSPECTIVE

Ethos is a Latin word that denotes the fundamental character or spirit of a community, group, or person. When used to discuss dramatic literature, ethos is that moral element used to determine a character's action rather than his or her thought or emotion. Ethos points to the inward being, to the moral fabric of the heart. In Biblical language, ethos absolutely compares to a person's heart. And our ethos, our heart, is important to God.

His Word tells us:

> Above all else, guard your heart,
> for everything you do flows from it.
> *Proverbs 4:23 NIV*

Above all else, guard your heart. Why? Because everything we do flows from the heart, from our inward being. And that "everything" includes leading women through God's Word. If we want to see women growing in authentic relationships with Christ and with one another, that process must first begin in our own hearts.

> For the Lord sees not as man sees: man looks on the
> outward appearance, but the Lord looks on the heart.
> *I Samuel 16:7*

So often, as individuals and as women's ministry groups, we get caught up in appearances. I'm guilty. How easy it is for us as leaders to dress ourselves up for Bible study, look nice on the outside, make sure the tables are inviting, share a few pleasant words, all the while never touching the core or the heart in order to make heart connections with God and with one another. God looks at the heart. Perhaps we should, too.

Truly, I believe that I could write a book concerning effectively "guarding our hearts" while leading women in inductive Bible study. However, for our purposes today, let's keep things simple and limit our necessary ingredients to three:
(1) Jesus
(2) Prayer
(3) The Word

By guarding our hearts in these ways, successful Bible study leadership is certain. Let's briefly understand.

GUARDING YOUR HEART WITH JESUS

This may seem so obvious, but honestly, isn't it easy for us to miss the forest for the trees? How can we expect our ladies to believe if we ourselves are not believing Jesus and His Word? Without Jesus and His Word dwelling in our hearts, we're not going to overflow with Him and His Spirit. Our efforts will certainly ring hollow. Paul puts it this way:

> If I speak in the tongues of men and of angels, but
> have not love, I am a noisy gong or a clanging cymbal.
> *I Corinthians 13:1*

None of us wants to annoy others as a gong gone wrong. But without a personal heart connection to His heart of love, we labor in our own strength. One of my leaders referred to this kind of fruit as being like the "fake grapes" found in her Grandma's kitchen. Rather, we are after the juicy sweet fruit of the Spirit that comes from abiding in the True Vine. To overflow with Christ, one must first abide in Him:

> Abide in me, and I in you. As the branch cannot
> bear fruit by itself, unless it abides in the vine,
> neither can you, unless you abide in me.
> *John 15:4*

Abiding in Jesus is the secret, powerful ingredient to leading Bible study. Okay, maybe it's not so secret, but it is powerful! Some days we feel that heart connection with God and other days we do not, but we can know we are abiding when we are obeying and seeking to follow His will.

Are you daily abiding with The Word from the inside out? Our character and our inner lives ought to align with our outward appearance. There is nothing more effective than a woman leading others with a sanctified and authentic heart. This transformation happens as a woman applies Scripture, yields to God's will and allows for the Spirit's holy work to happen within her own heart. That leads to true beauty. It's attractive. Others will want to follow. Peter says it this way:

> Let your adorning be the hidden person of the heart
> with the imperishable beauty of a gentle and quiet spirit,
> which in God's sight is very precious.
> *I Peter 3:4*

GUARDING YOUR HEART WITH **PRAYER**

Here, again, the need for prayer is likely obvious, but sometimes when we get caught up in the details, we overlook the obvious. Pray, pray, and pray! If Jesus required prayer in order to remain united with the Father in both purpose and mission, surely we need it more. Prayer helps us to stay focused on Christ, the Good Shepherd who leads the way to green pastures. As we study His Word, we desire to follow Christ to these places that teem with His life and living water. However, without Christ to do the heavy lifting of paving the way and clearing the path, we will struggle to get there. And so, we pray.

Set aside time to pray for Bible study. If your schedule allows, before you begin leading this study, take one day away from other activities to commit the weeks ahead to Him.

Remember that prayer is simply sharing your heart and relating with God. It involves both speaking and listening. I find the acronym *P.R.A.Y.* to be useful, especially when praying in groups. This template allows groups to walk through four steps of prayer:

P	PRAISE	Acknowledge your dependence on Him; yield to His ways.

Blessed are those who have learned to acclaim you,
who walk in the light of your presence, Lord.
Psalm 89:15 NIV

Beginning a session with praise turns our hearts toward God. In a group setting, I find it effective to encourage short "popcorn prayers" of praise where women take turns utilizing simple words and phrases to worship God. For example:

- I praise You, God, as the Light of the world.
- Lord, You are Life.
- I praise You for You are mighty to save.
- You are the truth.

R	REPENT	Confess and agree with God concerning sin.

If we confess our sins, he is faithful and just to forgive
us our sins and to cleanse us from all unrighteousness.
I John 1:9

Offer group members a silent moment to allow for private confession.

A	ADORE	Admire and thank God for His ways.

Let us come into his presence with thanksgiving;
let us make a joyful noise to him with songs of praise!
Psalm 95:2

Thanksgiving is a beautiful way to end a Bible study session. Together, give thanks to the Lord for all that He has revealed.

Y	YIELD	Acknowledge your dependence on God. Yield to His ways.

Whoever abides in me and I in him, he it is that bears much
fruit, for apart from me you can do nothing. | *John 15:5*

Delight yourself in the Lord, and he will give you the
desires of your heart. | *Psalm 37:4*

With that, what sorts of things shall we *yield* to God? Here are a few ideas and ways to align with God's heart:

- May God be glorified through the study.
- May God's Will be accomplished in the hearts of women.
- May women know, believe, and abide in Christ.
- May women's hearts be united with His and with one another.
- May God offer protection from all distractions as women commit to studying God's Word.
- May God's Word transform hearts and lives, that women would be holy as He is holy.

GUARDING YOUR HEART WITH **THE WORD**
Read. Reflect. Remember His Word.

Whether teaching a large group or facilitating discussion in a small group, it's easy for leaders to fall into the trap of thinking that we need to have all of the right answers. Furthermore, we often feel the need to be able to speak all those answers eloquently. Due to this false thinking, many leaders spend countless hours scouring commentaries. And we wear ourselves out! After all, God's Word is so deep and rich that we will not plumb the depths of a Scripture passage in just one week. Thinking we need to have all the right answers is a fallacy.

Yes! Without a doubt, commentaries have their valuable place for solid interpretation. (Interpretation is that portion of inductive study where women should all be on the same page.) However, the risk to leaders who spend too much time delving into their commentaries is that the workbook journals plus the teaching and discussion times will reflect the commentaries versus the scripture itself.

To counter this, we simply need time in God's Word. As we read, observe and marinate in the Bible text itself, God's Spirit teaches and leads. His Word speaks on its own. It's powerful and effective. We can trust in it!

So shall my word be that goes out from my mouth:
it shall not return to me empty, but it shall
accomplish that which I purpose, and
shall succeed in the thing for which I sent it.
Isaiah 55:11

Read, read, and read again. Read the daily Scripture passage using various translations. Read aloud, and read slowly. Ponder. Listen to the Word while driving. Talk about what you are learning and discovering in the Word with family and friends. This will help you be prepared to speak it when time for Bible study. Just as we marinate meat to soften, tenderize, and flavor it, we "sit in" the text allowing God's Spirit to soften, tenderize and flavor our hearts and minds with His personal message.

I have stored up your word in my heart,
that I might not sin against you.
Psalm 119:11

A challenging but brilliant way to soak in Scripture is memorization. Memorization is hard work, but the payoff is great. Scripture becomes embedded within us and can overflow from the heart when needed. Certainly, those Scriptures guard my own heart. And in leading, I have noticed that reciting Scripture over women deeply touches their hearts in a way that nothing else does.

Ideally, when studying in groups, teachers and small group leaders should prepare the study a week ahead of time. Yep! You read that right. Seek to be one week ahead of the regular study schedule. Then, allow time for leaders to review together before leading and teaching in groups the following week. The benefits of discussing, sharing, and grappling with the Word as leaders are priceless for preparation and confidence in leading. Also, through that time, God will knit together the hearts of the leaders. That dynamic will then transform the ethos or heart of the group as a whole.

Guarding hearts with Jesus, prayer, and His Word prepares us for life-changing and dynamic conversations around our Bible study tables. In fact, by communing with Jesus and His Spirit through prayer and His Word, you truly have all you need in order to successfully lead a group.

> But you will receive power when the Holy Spirit
> has come upon you, and you will be my witnesses
> in Jerusalem and in all Judea and Samaria,
> and to the end of the earth.
> *Acts 1:8*

The following tools and resources included in this appendix may provide additional help and support as you endeavor to lead your group. Use them however you find them to be helpful.

- Effective Leadership Guide
- Weekly Preparation Guide
- Bible Study Schedule
- Small Group Roster
- Attendance Record
- Prayer Log

effective *leadership*

A GUIDE TO LEADING A SMALL GROUP EFFECTIVELY

Remember that the goal for our study is to see women growing in relationship with Christ and one another. You do not need to be a Bible expert to lead women in discussion about His Word. You only need a heart to love and encourage women. So, what does effective small group leadership look like?

ENCOURAGING | In an *encouraging* small group, all participants feel included and welcome to share freely. Thoughts and ideas are respected, and women are cheered on in their efforts to grow closer to God through their study of His Word.

BIBLICALLY SOUND | When we endeavor to create a *biblically-sound* environment, we point women in the direction of truth and correct doctrine, gently guiding them away from wrong thinking.

BALANCED | In a group that is *balanced*, shy or quiet women are drawn out and encouraged to participate in discussions, while "over-sharers" are encouraged to listen to others and not to dominate the conversation.

WISE | A *wise* small group leader recognizes when the conversation is getting off-topic or veering toward gossip. In such situations, it is a good idea to redirect women back to the ultimate focus of the meeting: God's Word.

PRAYERFUL | A *prayerful* group leader is an asset to her group. She prays regularly for her group members and facilitates opportunities for them to pray for one another.

CONFIDENTIAL | Group members should feel secure that the things they share will remain *confidential*. An effective small group leader is committed to preserving the privacy of her group members.

weekly preparation guide
PREPARING FOR SMALL-GROUP MEETINGS

WEEK ONE | MEET PAUL

☐ Read the assigned daily passages.

☐ Use each daily framework to observe, interpret, and apply.

☐ Respond to all of the Day 5 questions.

☐ Pray for your small group meeting and for your group members.

1 What does this week's study tell me about God?	2 What does this week's study tell me about how I am to relate to Him?

WEEK TWO | GALATIANS 1

☐ Read the assigned daily passages.

☐ Use each daily framework to observe, interpret, and apply.

☐ Respond to all of the Day 5 questions.

☐ Pray for your small group meeting and for your group members.

1 What does this week's study tell me about God?	2 What does this week's study tell me about how I am to relate to Him?

WEEK THREE | GALATIANS 2

- ☐ Read the assigned daily passages.
- ☐ Use each daily framework to observe, interpret, and apply.
- ☐ Respond to all of the Day 5 questions.
- ☐ Pray for your small group meeting and for your group members.

1 What does this week's study tell me about God?	2 What does this week's study tell me about how I am to relate to Him?

WEEK FOUR | GALATIANS 3

- ☐ Read the assigned daily passages.
- ☐ Use each daily framework to observe, interpret, and apply.
- ☐ Respond to all of the Day 5 questions.
- ☐ Pray for your small group meeting and for your group members.

1 What does this week's study tell me about God?	2 What does this week's study tell me about how I am to relate to Him?

WEEK FIVE | GALATIANS 4

☐ Read the assigned daily passages.

☐ Use each daily framework to observe, interpret, and apply.

☐ Respond to all of the Day 5 questions.

☐ Pray for your small group meeting and for your group members.

1 What does this week's study tell me about God?	2 What does this week's study tell me about how I am to relate to Him?

WEEK SIX | GALATIANS 5

☐ Read the assigned daily passages.

☐ Use each daily framework to observe, interpret, and apply.

☐ Respond to all of the Day 5 questions.

☐ Pray for your small group meeting and for your group members.

1 What does this week's study tell me about God?	2 What does this week's study tell me about how I am to relate to Him?

WEEK SEVEN | GALATIANS 6

☐ Read the assigned daily passages.

☐ Use each daily framework to observe, interpret, and apply.

☐ Respond to all of the Day 5 questions.

☐ Respond to the "Wrapping Up" questions.

☐ Pray for your small group meeting and for your group members.

1 What does this week's study tell me about God?	2 What does this week's study tell me about how I am to relate to Him?

ALL SCRIPTURE IS BREATHED
OUT BY GOD AND PROFITABLE
FOR TEACHING, FOR REPROOF,
FOR CORRECTION, AND FOR
TRAINING IN RIGHTEOUSNESS,
THAT THE MAN OF GOD MAY
BE COMPLETE, EQUIPPED FOR
EVERY GOOD WORK.

2 TIMOTHY 3:16-17

bible study *schedule*

GALATIANS | A **SIMPLY BIBLE** STUDY

	READING ASSIGNMENT	SMALL GROUP MEETING DATE	LEADER MEETING DATE
WEEK 1			
WEEK 2			
WEEK 3			
WEEK 4			
WEEK 5			
WEEK 6			
WEEK 7			

small group *roster*

GALATIANS | A **SIMPLY BIBLE** STUDY

PARTICIPANT LIST

1
2
3
4
5
6
7
8
9
10
11
12
13

NAME	
BIRTHDAY	
PHONE NUMBER	
EMAIL ADDRESS	
CONTACT METHOD	
NOTES	

NAME

BIRTHDAY	
PHONE NUMBER	
EMAIL ADDRESS	
CONTACT METHOD	

NOTES

NAME

BIRTHDAY	
PHONE NUMBER	
EMAIL ADDRESS	
CONTACT METHOD	

NOTES

NAME

BIRTHDAY	
PHONE NUMBER	
EMAIL ADDRESS	
CONTACT METHOD	

NOTES

NAME	
BIRTHDAY	
PHONE NUMBER	
EMAIL ADDRESS	
CONTACT METHOD	
NOTES	

NAME	
BIRTHDAY	
PHONE NUMBER	
EMAIL ADDRESS	
CONTACT METHOD	
NOTES	

NAME	
BIRTHDAY	
PHONE NUMBER	
EMAIL ADDRESS	
CONTACT METHOD	
NOTES	

NAME

BIRTHDAY	
PHONE NUMBER	
EMAIL ADDRESS	
CONTACT METHOD	

NOTES

NAME

BIRTHDAY	
PHONE NUMBER	
EMAIL ADDRESS	
CONTACT METHOD	

NOTES

NAME

BIRTHDAY	
PHONE NUMBER	
EMAIL ADDRESS	
CONTACT METHOD	

NOTES

attendance *log*

GALATIANS | A **SIMPLY BIBLE** STUDY

PARTICIPANT'S NAME	WEEK 1 | MEET PAUL	WEEK 2 | GALATIANS 1	WEEK 3 | GALATIANS 2	WEEK 4 | GALATIANS 3	WEEK 5 | GALATIANS 4	WEEK 6 | GALATIANS 5	WEEK 7 | GALATIANS 6
1							
2							
3							
4							
5							
6							
7							
8							
9							
10							
11							
12							
13							

prayer *log*

GALATIANS | A **SIMPLY BIBLE** STUDY

DATE	NAME	REQUEST	FOLLOW-UP

DATE	NAME	REQUEST	FOLLOW-UP

DATE	NAME	REQUEST	FOLLOW-UP

DATE	NAME	REQUEST	FOLLOW-UP

DATE	NAME	REQUEST	FOLLOW-UP

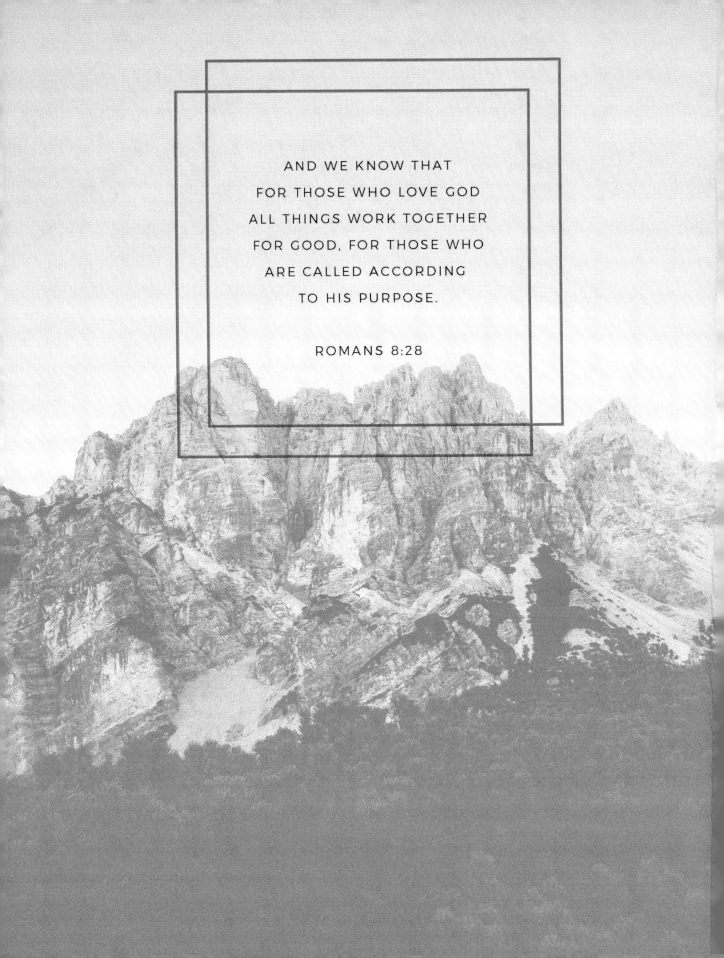

AND WE KNOW THAT
FOR THOSE WHO LOVE GOD
ALL THINGS WORK TOGETHER
FOR GOOD, FOR THOSE WHO
ARE CALLED ACCORDING
TO HIS PURPOSE.

ROMANS 8:28

Made in the USA
Columbia, SC
25 September 2023